The Dogs' Path of Life

WRITTEN AND ILLUSTRATED BY

CONSTANCE J. CHANDLEE

Balboa Press books may be ordered through booksellers or by contacting:

Balboa Press
A Division of Hay House
1663 Liberty Drive
Bloomington, IN 47403
www.balboapress.com
1 (877) 407-4847

ISBN: 978-1-5043-4289-6 (sc)
ISBN: 978-1-5043-4288-9 (e)

Library of Congress Control Number: 2015916713

Print information available on the last page.

Balboa Press rev. date: 11/24/2015

BALBOA
PRESS
A DIVISION OF HAY HOUSE

Contents

Introduction

We have learned a lot along our path of life.
Within these pages we share our thoughts
and pass them on to those that might
listen, and gain from what life has given.

Loving Oneself

I love me. There is no one like me.

I am beautiful, outside and inside.
I have my own talents and
that makes me special.

I value and respect myself.

It is important to take time for solitude. I get to observe, think, figure things out, and just be with me.

Each new moment is an opportunity
to be a better me. Sometimes, I set
goals to challenge myself. I don't always
succeed, but it is the process of the
path that leads me to a better me.

I can be a real goofball around others.
They say I am fun, positive, kind, and I
like to involve others in our groups.

Going to school is fun. I meet friends and
learn to understand what is being said to me.
The more I learn, the more fun I have.

Having a positive attitude is fun. It changes me, and my world.

I can do anything I put my heart and mind to.

I am grateful for being alive, and for my health, my ball, my food, my home, my family, my bed, and for going on walks and playing with friends. I am so grateful for what I have.

Health

Kisses
for
Food

Healthy foods give my body the nutrients it needs so I can play and be with those I love.

Hygiene is important to my health: brushing teeth, taking baths, and washing paws.

Get into a sport for the fun and exercise.
I love playing with my ball.

Laughter is the best medicine. Laughing
makes me feel so good. Laughter can
heal the mind, body, and heart.

Rest and sleep are good for the health of
my body and mind. I feel better, and I can
do my job at protecting the house and yard.
It makes me feel good to do my part.

Loved Ones

I am loved by others. And, it is a good idea to tell others that I love them; ...and to tell them often.

My mother fed me, watched over me, made sure that I didn't run into the street and said "NO" a lot. I realized later she just wanted to protect me from harm.

As I have taken interest in what my friends and family love to do, I have added fun experiences to my life. Spending time with those I love means more than anything else that I can do.

I love it when we get in the car and gooooooo!
It's an adventure. I have learned so much about
me and the world by stepping outside my yard.

I have toys that are dear to me. I have learned
that keeping one special gift from someone
I love means so much to me. And there is
less to put away at the end of the day.

Meeting someone new can be the beginning
of a new journey of love. Life is so much
better when sharing it with a friend.

It is so nice to find that someone special in life and to share it with them. It makes life more fun, and experiencing depth of love helps me grow.

How to Treat Others

I respect others who are different than me, and
I learn something from them about my world.

I let others know that I am there for them:
to listen, to guide, and to help. It is important
to be heard and to feel that one matters.

It is so much fun to make someone happy from just a smile. I can change the world around me!

Sometimes I need my space,... as others do too.

Sometimes When...

At times I felt alone or felt that I couldn't do something on my own. But all I had to do was ask for help and I would get it. That made me feel loved.

Sometimes, I need to forgive myself for something I wish that I did not do. I remind myself that I am here to learn, so I tell myself, "Learn from this, and do it differently next time."

I don't take myself seriously like I used to. I have learned to laugh at myself when I have done something silly, which I will do from time to time.

Sometimes I felt awkward and didn't seem to fit in with others. But, eventually I found my way. I discovered who I was and I became confident in life, and in myself.

When I don't know what to do, I
ask myself, "What do I want to do,"
and then I listen to my heart.

When I don't know which path to take,
I ask within for guidance, and then I
listen for my intuition to guide me.

When I set my fears aside, I
have more fun in life.

The World

I enjoy, respect, and love all of
nature and Mother Earth.

Whether in solitude or with others, I take
time to enjoy where I live and to respect it
by taking care of it. I enjoy the beach sand in
my toes, the smell of plants and flowers in my
nose. My eyes wonder at the mountains' and
lakes' beauty. Mother Earth is so wondrous.

I love the outdoors during the different seasons: the spring flowers to smell, the summer sun against my face, the fall leaves to play in, and the winter's snow to run in. Each has its beauty and wonder.

I love to sing from my heart, joy
and love into the world.

The Closing

I have lost loved ones and that is sad.
They live in my heart and I in theirs. I
have known love in my life and believe
we will be together again one day.

Life is the process along the
path, and it has no ending.

I love to give and to receive. I love to give kisses. I love to receive tummy rubs and a toss of a ball. Did someone say, "Where's the ball........?" Got to gooooooo!

We hope that you have enjoyed walking down our path of life and will think about what we have shared and might even pass our thoughts along. We think life might become a better place if we are nicer to ourselves,...to others,...and to Mother Earth.

Acknowledgements

I want to thank my husband, Tom Dorst,
for his idea for this book, his editing, and his support.

I also want to thank my friends Betty Bobu,
for her encouragement and guidance and
Lynn Deaton for her editing.

I would like to acknowledge the following women photographers who excel in their field and support the wellbeing of animals. Without their beautiful work, I would not have been inspired to learn water coloring from their photographs and been able to help raise funds and attention for non-profit animal organizations in my area. Some of those paintings are included within this book.

Amanda Jones Photography at www.amandajones.com/
Amanda is seen in numerous magazines and at her studio in North Adams, Ma., and schedules photo sessions nationwide.

Portia Shao at www.PositiveVista.com/
Portia helps our Santa Cruz SPCA in the effort of getting animals adopted with her time, expertise, and photography.

About the Author

Constance has won nationwide and worldwide awards through her creativity and excellence in sewing. She has been featured in magazines and was once honored by placement on a magazine front cover when she won "Best of Show" in a national contest.

Constance turned her talent to helping animal nonprofits through her watercolor dog art to raise funds and attention to shelter animals. Her artwork has been featured in numerous local events and event advertisements. She brings her artwork and spiritual growth learning and teaching together in her book through her love for dogs.

Horses, dogs, cats, and rabbits have also been benefited through her animal communication, clear quartz crystal work, and her knowledge of Linda Tellington's TTouch body and groundwork techniques.

Constance lives with her husband and their two dogs in Santa Cruz, California.

Printed in the United States
By Bookmasters